HOW TO BECOME A SUCCESSFUL FREELANCER

OLORUNNISOLA OLALEKAN & AYODELE CHRISTOPHER

To all the aspiring freelancers who dare to dream, embrace their passions, and pursue a life of freedom and success. Your determination and relentless pursuit of excellence inspire us all. May this book serve as a guiding light on your journey to becoming a successful freelancer.

CONTENTS

CHAPTER 1: INTRODUCTION TO FREELANCING

1.1 The Freelancing Revolution

The world of work has undergone a significant transformation in recent years, and one of the most prominent shifts is the rise of freelancing. The traditional model of employment, with its 9-to-5 office routine and long-term job security, is no longer the only path to success. Freelancing, also known as independent contracting or self-employment, has emerged as a viable alternative for individuals seeking greater autonomy, flexibility, and control over their professional lives.

The freelancing revolution can be attributed to several factors. Technological advancements have made it easier than ever to connect with clients and collaborate remotely. The internet has opened up a global marketplace, allowing freelancers to work with clients from different parts of the world. Moreover, the gig economy has gained momentum, with companies increasingly relying on freelance talent to meet their specialized needs.

Freelancing offers a multitude of benefits that attract professionals from various industries. One of the most significant advantages is the ability to be your own boss. As a freelancer, you have the freedom to choose your clients, projects, and working hours. You can shape your career according to your preferences, focusing on the areas that excite you the most. This level of control over your professional life can lead to increased job satisfaction and a stronger sense of fulfillment.

Additionally, freelancing provides flexibility that is often absent in traditional employment. You have the power to set your own schedule, work from anywhere with an internet connection, and take breaks whenever you need them. This flexibility allows you to achieve a better work-life balance, accommodate personal commitments, and pursue other passions alongside your freelancing career.

Another allure of freelancing is the potential for higher earning potential. As a freelancer, you have the opportunity to negotiate your rates and take on multiple projects simultaneously. With the right skills, expertise, and marketing strategy, you can command higher fees and increase your income. Moreover, freelancers can take advantage of tax deductions and expense write-offs, potentially reducing their tax burden.

The freelancing revolution has also been fueled by changing attitudes towards work. Many individuals now prioritize meaningful work experiences, personal fulfillment, and the pursuit of their passions. Freelancing allows you to choose the projects and clients that align with your values and interests. You have the freedom to specialize in areas that you are passionate about and build a portfolio that reflects your expertise.

However, it's important to note that freelancing is not without its challenges. Freelancers often face uncertainty regarding a steady income, the need for self-promotion and client acquisition, and the responsibility of managing their own business affairs. It requires discipline, self-motivation, and adaptability to succeed as a freelancer.

1.2 Why Choose Freelancing?

The decision to become a freelancer is a personal one, and it's essential to consider the reasons behind your choice. Understanding your motivations will not only help you stay committed but also enable you to tailor your freelancing journey to align with your goals.

Financial Independence: Freelancing can offer the potential for higher income compared to traditional employment. As a freelancer, you have control over your rates and can take on multiple projects to maximize your earnings. The ability to determine your own financial destiny is a compelling reason for many individuals to pursue a freelancing career.

Flexibility and Work-Life Balance: If you value flexibility in your work arrangements and desire a better work-life balance, freelancing can be an ideal choice. As a freelancer, you have the freedom to set your own schedule, choose where you work from, and manage your time according to your needs. This flexibility allows you to prioritize personal commitments, spend more time with loved ones, and pursue hobbies and interests outside of work. It grants you the autonomy to design your work-life integration in a way that suits your unique circumstances.

Personal Fulfillment: Freelancing provides an opportunity to pursue your passions and engage in work that truly fulfills you. Unlike traditional employment, where you may be restricted to a specific role or industry, freelancing allows you to explore diverse projects and work with clients across various fields. This freedom to choose work that aligns with your interests and values can lead to a greater sense of personal satisfaction and fulfillment.

Professional Growth and Development: As a freelancer, you have the chance to continuously expand your skill set and expertise. Each project presents a new challenge, allowing you to learn and acquire new knowledge. You can take on projects that push you outside of your comfort zone, fostering personal and professional growth. Additionally, freelancing exposes you to different clients, industries, and perspectives, broadening your horizons and enhancing your marketability.

Diverse Work Experience: Freelancing offers a dynamic work experience that can be highly rewarding. The variety of projects and clients you encounter as a freelancer exposes you to different work environments, cultures, and business practices. This exposure builds adaptability, resilience, and the ability to work with diverse stakeholders. It also allows you to build a portfolio of work that showcases your versatility and capabilities.

Entrepreneurial Spirit: Freelancing nurtures an entrepreneurial mindset and encourages self-reliance. As a freelancer, you are not just providing a service; you are running your own business. This entrepreneurial aspect of freelancing allows you to develop business skills, such as marketing, networking, and financial management. You have the opportunity to build a personal brand, cultivate professional relationships, and create a sustainable freelancing business.

1.3 Is Freelancing Right for You?

While freelancing offers numerous benefits, it's important to assess whether it is the right fit for your personality, lifestyle, and career goals. Freelancing requires a specific set of characteristics and skills to thrive in this unique work environment. Consider the following factors to determine if freelancing is suitable for you:

Self-Motivation and Discipline: Freelancing requires a high level of self-motivation and discipline. As a freelancer, you are responsible for managing your time, setting goals, and meeting deadlines without the structure of a traditional workplace. You must be able to stay focused, organized, and driven even when faced with distractions or challenges.

Adaptability and Resilience: Freelancers often encounter a constantly changing work landscape. Clients, projects, and market demands can fluctuate, requiring you to adapt quickly and embrace new opportunities. It's crucial to be resilient in the face of setbacks, rejection, and uncertainty. The ability to bounce back, learn from failures, and persist in the pursuit of your goals is essential for freelancers.

Effective Communication: Strong communication skills are paramount in freelancing. As a freelancer, you'll be interacting with clients, collaborators, and stakeholders remotely. Clear and concise communication, both written and verbal, is vital for understanding project requirements, managing expectations, and building strong professional relationships. Active listening and the ability to convey your ideas effectively are crucial for successful freelancing.

Financial Management: Freelancing involves managing your finances independently. You'll need to set appropriate rates, track income and expenses, invoice clients, and plan for taxes. A basic understanding of financial management and budgeting is essential to ensure your freelancing career is financially sustainable.

Risk Tolerance: Freelancing inherently involves a degree of risk and uncertainty. Unlike traditional employment, there may not be a steady paycheck or job security. Freelancers often experience fluctuations in income and must be comfortable with the unpredictable nature of the freelance market. Assess your risk tolerance and ability to handle financial variability before committing to freelancing.

Desire for Continuous Learning: Freelancing necessitates a mindset of continuous learning and improvement. To thrive as a freelancer, you must be open to acquiring new skills, staying updated with industry trends, and adapting to evolving client needs. The willingness to invest time and effort in your professional development is crucial for long-term success in freelancing.

Workstyle Compatibility: Reflect on your preferred workstyle and environment. Freelancing offers the freedom to work from anywhere, but it also requires self-motivation and the ability to work independently. Consider if you thrive in a structured office environment or if you prefer the flexibility of remote work. Assess your work preferences and determine if freelancing aligns with your preferred workstyle.

Networking and Self-Promotion: Freelancers often need to actively network and market their services to attract clients. Building a strong professional network, showcasing your expertise, and promoting your services are essential aspects of freelancing. Evaluate your comfort level with networking, self-promotion, and marketing activities to gauge if freelancing is a suitable choice for you.

1.4 Setting Your Freelancing Goals

To embark on a successful freelancing journey, it is crucial to set clear and achievable goals. Setting goals provides direction, motivation, and a framework for measuring your progress. Consider the following steps when setting your freelancing goals:

Define Your Vision: Start by envisioning your ideal freelancing career. What does success look like to you? Identify the lifestyle, income level, and professional achievements you aspire to attain. This vision will serve as a guiding light as you navigate your freelancing journey.

Set SMART Goals: SMART goals are specific, measurable, achievable, relevant, and time-bound. Break down your overarching vision into smaller, actionable goals that meet these criteria. For example, if your vision is to earn a certain income level, a SMART goal could be to increase your average project rate by a specific percentage within the next six months. SMART goals provide clarity and focus, making it easier to track your progress.

Prioritize Your Goals: It's essential to prioritize your goals based on their significance and urgency. Determine which goals will have the most significant impact on your freelancing career and focus on those first. This approach ensures that you are allocating your time and resources effectively.

Create an Action Plan: Once you have identified your goals, develop a detailed action plan to achieve them. Break each goal into smaller tasks or milestones and assign deadlines to each. This step-by-step plan will help you stay organized and motivated as you work towards your objectives.

Monitor and Adjust: Regularly monitor your progress towards your goals and make adjustments as needed. Assess what is working well and what needs improvement. Be open to adapting your action plan or revising your goals if necessary. Freelancing is a dynamic journey, and it's essential to be flexible and responsive to changes in the market or your own circumstances.

Celebrate Milestones: Acknowledge and celebrate your achievements along the way. Celebrating milestones, no matter how small, boosts your morale, reinforces your progress, and keeps you motivated. Recognize your hard work and use it as fuel to propel you towards further success.

Remember, goal setting is an ongoing process. As you achieve your initial goals, set new ones to continue challenging yourself and pushing your freelancing career to new heights. Regularly revisit and reassess your goals to ensure they align with your evolving vision and aspirations.

By understanding the freelancing revolution, assessing your suitability for freelancing, and setting clear goals, you are laying a solid foundation for your freelancing journey. As you proceed through this book, we will delve deeper into various aspects of freelancing, providing valuable insights, strategies, and practical tips to support your path to becoming a successful freelancer.

CHAPTER 2: BUILDING A STRONG FOUNDATION

2.1 Assessing Your Skills and Expertise

As you embark on your journey to become a successful freelancer, one of the first steps is to assess your skills and expertise. Freelancing allows you to capitalize on your unique abilities and offer them as services to clients who are seeking your particular skill set. By understanding your strengths and areas of expertise, you can position yourself as a valuable asset in the freelance marketplace.

To begin, take some time to reflect on the skills you possess. Consider your educational background, work experience, and any specialized training you have received. Make a list of your strengths, both technical and soft skills. Technical skills are specific to certain industries or professions, such as web development, graphic design, or writing. Soft skills, on the other hand, refer to personal attributes like communication, time management, and problem-solving abilities.

Once you have identified your skills, it's important to evaluate your level of expertise in each area. Determine your proficiency, experience, and any certifications or qualifications you may have. Be honest with yourself during this assessment, as it will help you understand where you excel and where you may need further development.

Technical skills can be assessed by reviewing your previous work experience, projects, and the feedback you've received from clients or colleagues. If you are just starting out and lack professional experience, consider taking online courses or completing freelance projects to gain practical knowledge and build your portfolio.

Soft skills are equally important in freelancing as they contribute to your overall professionalism and client satisfaction. Assess your ability to communicate effectively, meet deadlines, handle client feedback, and manage your time efficiently. Identify areas where you can improve and seek resources, such as books, courses, or online tutorials, to enhance these skills.

In addition to assessing your skills, consider your passions and interests. Freelancing offers the opportunity to do work that you truly enjoy, so identifying your niche will play a vital role in your success. Think about the industries or topics that genuinely excite you. By aligning your skills with your passions, you can create a more fulfilling and rewarding freelancing career.

Once you have assessed your skills, expertise, and identified your passions, you can determine the specific services you will offer as a freelancer. This clarity will help you target the right clients and position yourself as an expert in your chosen field.

Remember that skills and expertise can be developed and expanded over time. As you gain more experience and knowledge, you can continuously assess and refine your skill set. Stay updated with the latest industry trends, technologies, and best practices to ensure you are offering high-quality services to your clients. Never stop learning and seeking opportunities for growth.

2.2 Identifying Your Niche

Now that you have assessed your skills and expertise, it's time to identify your niche. A niche is a specialized segment of the market that you will focus on as a freelancer. By narrowing down your target audience and the type of work you offer, you can position yourself as an expert in a particular field, making it easier to attract clients and stand out from the competition.

Identifying your niche is essential for several reasons. Firstly, it helps you tailor your services to meet the specific needs and preferences of your target audience. By specializing in a particular area, you can develop a deep understanding of your clients' pain points and deliver solutions that directly address their challenges.

Secondly, narrowing down your niche allows you to position yourself as an authority or expert in that field. Clients are more likely to choose a freelancer who specializes in their industry or has extensive experience in solving the specific problems they face. Being seen as an expert not only increases your credibility but also enables you to charge higher rates for your services.

To identify your niche, consider the intersection between your skills, expertise, and personal interests. Look for areas where you have a unique advantage or where there is a demand for your specific skills. Conduct market research to identify trends and opportunities within your chosen field. This will help you understand the market demand and the needs of potential clients.

Start by examining your existing skill set and experience. Are there particular skills or areas in which you excel? Can you identify any patterns or themes in your previous work or projects? These insights can guide you towards potential niches that align with your strengths.

Consider your interests and passions as well. Think about the industries or topics that genuinely excite you. Are there any specific areas where you can combine your skills and expertise with your personal interests? This alignment can provide you with a sense of fulfillment and enjoyment in your freelancing career.

Research the market to identify potential niches that are in demand. Look for gaps or underserved areas where your skills and expertise can fill a need. Explore online forums, industry-specific websites, and social media groups to gain insights into the challenges and pain points faced by your target audience.

Networking with professionals in your chosen field can also provide valuable information and potential collaborations. Attend industry events, participate in webinars, or join online communities where you can connect with peers and learn from their experiences.

It's important to strike a balance when choosing your niche. While it's important to be specific enough to differentiate yourself from general freelancers, it's also crucial to have a niche broad enough to provide a sustainable client base. For example, instead of being a "freelance writer," you could specialize in "health and wellness content writing" or "technical writing for the software industry." By narrowing down your focus, you can position yourself as an expert in a specific domain, allowing you to charge higher rates and attract clients who value your expertise.

Once you have identified your niche, it's time to develop a marketing strategy tailored to that specific audience. This includes creating targeted content, building a network within your niche, and positioning yourself as a go-to expert in your field. With a well-defined niche, you can differentiate yourself in a crowded market and attract clients who are specifically seeking the skills and expertise you offer.

2.3 Developing a Personal Brand

In the competitive world of freelancing, building a strong personal brand is essential. Your personal brand represents your professional identity and what sets you apart from other freelancers. It is how you communicate your unique value proposition to potential clients. Developing a strong personal brand will help you establish credibility, attract your target audience, and ultimately win more freelance opportunities.

To start building your personal brand, define your brand identity. Consider your values, mission, and the message you want to convey to your audience. Think about the qualities and characteristics that make you stand out as a freelancer. Are you known for your creativity, reliability, or exceptional customer service? Identifying these key attributes will help shape your brand identity.

Begin by conducting a self-audit. Reflect on your strengths, skills, and unique selling points. What makes you different from other freelancers in your industry? How do you want to be perceived by clients? Understanding your unique strengths will form the foundation of your personal brand.

Next, research your target audience. Understand their needs, pain points, and preferences. This knowledge will help you tailor your brand messaging and create content that resonates with your potential clients. The better you understand your audience, the more effectively you can position yourself as the solution to their problems.

Craft a compelling brand story that showcases your journey and highlights your expertise. Share your background, experiences, and milestones that have shaped your freelancing career. Emphasize how your unique skills and perspective benefit your clients. Your brand story should be authentic, relatable, and compelling, connecting with your audience on a deeper level.

Visual branding is another important aspect of building your personal brand. Design a professional logo, choose a consistent color palette, and select fonts that reflect your brand personality. These visual elements should be integrated across your website, social media profiles, business cards, and any other marketing materials. Consistency in visual branding helps create a memorable and cohesive brand image.

Your branding efforts should also extend to your communication style. Develop a consistent tone of voice that reflects your brand personality. Whether it's friendly, professional, or conversational, make sure it aligns with your target audience and the services you offer.

In addition to visual and verbal elements, your personal brand should emphasize your expertise and showcase your unique selling points. Share your knowledge and insights through blog posts, social media content, or even guest contributions to industry publications. Position yourself as a thought leader by providing valuable information and engaging with your audience.

Building a personal brand also involves building a network of professional relationships. Connect with fellow freelancers, industry experts, and potential clients through networking events, online communities, and social media platforms. Engage in meaningful conversations, offer support and advice, and collaborate on projects whenever possible. These connections can lead to referrals and opportunities for growth.

Remember that building a personal brand is an ongoing process. Continuously monitor and evaluate your brand's effectiveness, adapting and refining as necessary. Solicit feedback from clients and peers to gain insights into how your brand is perceived and make adjustments accordingly. Your personal brand should evolve as you grow as a freelancer and as the market changes.

By developing a strong personal brand, you can differentiate yourself in a competitive freelancing landscape, attract your target audience, and build long-term relationships with clients who value your unique skills and expertise.

2.4 Creating a Professional Portfolio

One of the most powerful tools in a freelancer's arsenal is a well-crafted professional portfolio. A portfolio showcases your best work, demonstrates your skills and expertise, and provides potential clients with tangible evidence of your abilities. Creating an impressive portfolio is crucial for establishing credibility and winning new freelance opportunities.

Start by selecting a variety of your best work samples that highlight different aspects of your skills and expertise. If you're just starting out and don't have much professional experience, consider creating sample projects that demonstrate your capabilities. For example, if you're a graphic designer, design a hypothetical logo or create a mock website to showcase your design skills.

When curating your portfolio, focus on quality over quantity. Choose a select few pieces that are relevant to your niche and demonstrate the range of services you offer. Ensure that your portfolio is visually appealing and easy to navigate. Use high-resolution images, clear descriptions, and consider incorporating client testimonials or case studies to provide additional validation.

In addition to showcasing completed projects, consider including works in progress or personal passion projects that demonstrate your ongoing growth and dedication to your craft. This shows potential clients that you are continually refining your skills and staying up to date with industry trends.

Your portfolio should have a prominent online presence. Create a professional website or utilize dedicated portfolio platforms to showcase your work. Optimize your portfolio for search engines by including relevant keywords and meta tags. Regularly update your portfolio with new projects and remove outdated or less representative work to maintain its relevance and freshness.

Consider creating a compelling "About Me" page that provides insights into your background, expertise, and values. This personal touch can help potential clients connect with you on a deeper level and understand your unique perspective.

When presenting your portfolio to potential clients, tailor it to their specific needs and industry. Highlight projects that align with their business or showcase your understanding of their target audience. Customizing your portfolio demonstrates your ability to deliver solutions that are relevant and valuable to their specific requirements.

Don't forget to include contact information and clear call-to-action buttons or links throughout your portfolio. Make it easy for potential clients to reach out to you for inquiries or project proposals. Promptly respond to inquiries and maintain professionalism in all your interactions.

Regularly update your portfolio with new projects, skills, and client testimonials. As you complete new projects or gain additional expertise, incorporate them into your portfolio to showcase your growth and versatility. This ongoing refinement ensures that your portfolio remains up to date and reflects your current capabilities.

Remember that your portfolio is a dynamic tool that should evolve with your freelancing career. Continuously seek feedback from clients, peers, and mentors to improve the presentation and effectiveness of your portfolio. Strive to consistently deliver high-quality work that exceeds client expectations, as your portfolio is a reflection of your professional capabilities.

2.5 Setting Up Your Freelancing Workspace

As a freelancer, your workspace plays a crucial role in your productivity and overall success. Whether you work from home, a co-working space, or a dedicated office, setting up an efficient and inspiring workspace is essential for staying focused and maximizing your output.

First and foremost, designate a specific area solely for work. Having a dedicated workspace helps create a separation between your personal life and your freelancing career. It allows you to mentally switch into work mode and helps minimize distractions. Ideally, choose a quiet and well-lit space with minimal interruptions.

Invest in essential equipment and tools that align with your freelancing services. This could include a reliable computer, software, peripherals, and any industry-specific equipment. Consider ergonomics and prioritize a comfortable chair, an ergonomic keyboard, and a monitor positioned at eye level to support good posture and reduce the risk of injuries.

Organize your workspace in a way that promotes efficiency and minimizes clutter. Use storage solutions, such as shelves, drawers, or file cabinets, to keep your supplies, documents, and equipment neatly organized and easily accessible. Implement a filing system for both physical and digital files to ensure efficient retrieval and organization.

Maintain a clean and tidy workspace to create a conducive environment for productivity. Regularly declutter your desk and remove any unnecessary items. A clean workspace not only improves focus but also creates a sense of calm and order.

Personalize your workspace with items that inspire and motivate you. Decorate with plants, artwork, or meaningful objects that reflect your personality and provide a sense of comfort. Consider incorporating a vision board or a motivational quote to keep you focused on your goals.

Ensure that your workspace is equipped with a reliable internet connection to facilitate seamless communication with clients, access to online resources, and efficient file transfers. Invest in a backup system to protect your work and important files from potential data loss.

Establish a daily routine and set boundaries to maintain a healthy work-life balance. Determine your working hours and stick to them as much as possible. Communicate your availability to clients and set clear expectations regarding response times and project deadlines.

Additionally, create a system for organizing your tasks and projects. Utilize project management tools, to-do lists, or digital calendars to keep track of deadlines, prioritize tasks, and stay on top of your workload. This will help you maintain focus, meet client expectations, and avoid unnecessary stress.

Lastly, remember to take care of yourself while working from your freelance workspace. Prioritize breaks, exercise, and proper nutrition to ensure your well-being. Incorporate regular physical activity and practice self-care techniques to avoid burnout and maintain a healthy work-life balance.

In conclusion, building a strong foundation as a freelancer is crucial for long-term success. Assessing your skills and expertise allows you to understand your strengths and areas for improvement. Identifying your niche helps you differentiate yourself in the market and attract clients who value your specialized services. Developing a personal brand establishes your professional identity and positions you as an expert. Creating a professional portfolio showcases your best work and builds credibility. Finally, setting up a well-organized and inspiring workspace promotes productivity and supports your overall well-being.

By focusing on these foundational aspects, you will lay the groundwork for a thriving freelancing career. In the next chapter, we will explore the strategies and techniques for finding and attracting clients, establishing a strong online presence, and managing your freelance business effectively.

CHAPTER 3: ESTABLISHING YOUR ONLINE PRESENCE

In today's digital age, establishing a strong online presence is essential for freelancers to reach a wider audience, showcase their work, and attract potential clients. Your online presence serves as a virtual storefront, where you can showcase your skills, build credibility, and communicate your unique value proposition. In this chapter, we will explore the key strategies and techniques to establish a compelling online presence as a freelancer.

3.1 Crafting an Effective Freelancer Website

A well-designed and informative website is the cornerstone of your online presence as a freelancer. It serves as a hub for potential clients to learn more about your services, view your portfolio, and contact you for inquiries. Crafting an effective freelancer website is crucial for making a strong first impression and converting visitors into clients.

Start by choosing a professional domain name that reflects your brand identity and is easy to remember. Register your domain name and secure reliable web hosting to ensure your website is accessible and performs well. Consider using your name or a variation of it in the domain to establish a personal connection with your audience.

When designing your website, prioritize simplicity, functionality, and user experience. Choose a clean and modern layout that is easy to navigate. Include clear and concise information about your services, skills, and expertise. Use high-quality images, graphics, and typography that align with your brand personality.

Craft a compelling "About Me" page that showcases your background, experience, and unique selling points. Share your story, including how you got started as a freelancer and what sets you apart from others in your field. Use this opportunity to establish trust and connect with potential clients on a personal level.

Create a dedicated page to showcase your portfolio, highlighting your best work samples that align with your niche. Provide brief descriptions of each project, emphasizing the challenges you faced and the solutions you delivered. Include testimonials or case studies from satisfied clients to further validate your skills and expertise.

Make sure your website is optimized for search engines (SEO). Conduct keyword research to identify relevant keywords related to your services and industry. Incorporate these keywords naturally throughout your website, including in page titles, headings, content, and meta tags. This will help improve your website's visibility in search engine results and attract organic traffic.

Include clear and prominent contact information on your website, such as a contact form, email address, and phone number. Make it easy for potential clients to reach out to you with inquiries or project proposals. Respond to inquiries promptly and maintain professionalism in all your interactions.

Regularly update your website with new projects, blog posts, or industry insights to demonstrate your ongoing growth and expertise. This shows potential clients that you are actively engaged in your field and up to date with the latest industry trends.

Lastly, ensure that your website is mobile-friendly and responsive. With the increasing use of mobile devices, it's crucial that your website looks and functions seamlessly across different screen sizes. Test your website on various devices to ensure a consistent and optimized user experience.

By crafting an effective freelancer website, you establish a professional online presence that showcases your skills, expertise, and unique value proposition. Your website becomes a powerful tool for attracting potential clients and converting them into paying projects.

3.2 Optimizing Your Online Profiles

In addition to your website, optimizing your online profiles on various platforms is essential for building a strong online presence as a freelancer. Online profiles provide additional visibility and credibility, allowing potential clients to find and learn more about you. Here are some key platforms to focus on when optimizing your online profiles.

1. Professional Networking Platforms: Platforms like LinkedIn are invaluable for freelancers. Create a compelling profile that highlights your skills, experience, and accomplishments. Use a professional profile picture and craft a compelling headline that captures attention. Write a concise and engaging summary that showcases your expertise and includes relevant keywords. Connect with other professionals, join relevant groups, and actively engage with the community by sharing valuable insights and participating in discussions.

2. Freelance Platforms: If you choose to use freelance platforms such as Upwork, Fiverr, or Freelancer, optimize your profile to stand out from the competition. Complete your profile with relevant information, including your skills, experience, and portfolio samples. Craft a persuasive profile description that clearly communicates the value you provide to clients. Showcase positive client feedback and ratings to build credibility. Proactively apply for relevant projects and maintain professionalism in your interactions with clients.

3. Social Media Platforms: Leverage social media platforms like Facebook, Twitter, Instagram, and Pinterest to establish your presence and engage with your target audience. Choose platforms that align with your target market and industry. Optimize your profiles by using consistent branding elements such as profile pictures, cover photos, and bios that reflect your personal brand. Share valuable content, industry insights, and updates about your projects. Engage with your audience by responding to comments, participating in relevant discussions, and networking with peers and potential clients.

4. Industry-Specific Platforms: Depending on your niche, explore industry-specific platforms and online communities relevant to your field. For example, if you're a web developer, consider participating in forums like Stack Overflow or GitHub to showcase your expertise and contribute to the community. Engage in discussions, answer questions, and share your knowledge to establish yourself as an authority in your niche.

When optimizing your online profiles, consistency is key. Use consistent branding elements, such as profile pictures, logos, and taglines, across different platforms. Ensure that the information provided on each platform is accurate, up to date, and consistent with your personal brand and website.

Regularly monitor and manage your online profiles. Respond promptly to inquiries or messages, and maintain professionalism in your interactions. Actively seek endorsements or recommendations from satisfied clients to build credibility and trust.

By optimizing your online profiles, you expand your reach and increase your visibility in the digital landscape. Potential clients can find you more easily, learn about your skills and expertise, and be motivated to reach out to you for freelance opportunities.

3.3 Leveraging Social Media for Freelancing Success

Social media platforms offer a powerful avenue for freelancers to connect with their target audience, build brand awareness, and attract potential clients. When utilized effectively, social media can be a valuable tool for freelancing success. Here are some key strategies to leverage social media for your freelance business.

1. Choose the Right Platforms: Identify the social media platforms that align with your target audience and industry. For example, if you're a visual artist or photographer, platforms like Instagram or Pinterest may be ideal for showcasing your work. If you provide professional services or B2B solutions, platforms like LinkedIn or Twitter may be more suitable. Focus your efforts on the platforms where your target clients are most active.

2. Develop a Consistent Brand Voice: Establish a consistent brand voice across your social media profiles. Determine the tone and style that aligns with your brand identity and target audience. Whether it's friendly, professional, humorous, or informative, ensure that your brand voice resonates with your ideal clients. Consistency in your brand voice helps build recognition and trust among your followers.

3. Share Valuable Content: Create and curate content that is valuable and relevant to your target audience. Share industry insights, tips, tutorials, or thought leadership articles that showcase your expertise. Engage your followers by asking questions, encouraging discussions, and responding to comments. By consistently providing value, you position yourself as a trusted resource in your field.

4. Visual Storytelling: Visual content is highly engaging and can significantly impact your social media presence. Share eye-catching images, videos, or infographics that represent your work and capture the attention of your audience. Use compelling visuals to tell stories, evoke emotions, and communicate your brand message effectively.

5. Hashtags and Keywords: Utilize hashtags and keywords strategically to

expand your reach and visibility. Research and use relevant hashtags that are popular within your industry or niche. Incorporate keywords naturally in your social media posts to optimize discoverability. Engage with others using the same hashtags, and participate in industry-related conversations to expand your network.

6. Networking and Collaboration: Social media platforms provide excellent opportunities for networking and collaboration. Connect with other freelancers, industry influencers, and potential clients. Engage in conversations, share each other's content, and collaborate on projects or campaigns. Building relationships on social media can lead to referrals, partnerships, and valuable connections.

7. Paid Advertising: Consider investing in paid advertising on social media platforms to amplify your reach and target specific demographics. Platforms like Facebook, Instagram, and LinkedIn offer targeted advertising options that allow you to reach your ideal clients. Set clear goals, define your target audience, and optimize your ad campaigns for maximum effectiveness.

8. Analytics and Measurement: Monitor and analyze your social media performance using platform-specific analytics tools or third-party tools. Track key metrics such as engagement, reach, click-through rates, and conversions. Use these insights to understand what content resonates with your audience, refine your social media strategy, and make data-driven decisions to optimize your efforts.

Remember, consistency and authenticity are key to social media success. Engage with your audience regularly, respond to comments and messages, and stay true to your brand values. Social media is a long-term investment, so be patient and persistent in building your presence and nurturing relationships.

3.4 Showcasing Your Work and Expertise Online

One of the most effective ways to establish your online presence as a freelancer is by showcasing your work and expertise. Clients want to see tangible evidence of your skills and capabilities before they hire you. By effectively showcasing your work and expertise online, you can build credibility, attract potential clients, and differentiate yourself from the competition. Here are key strategies to showcase your work and expertise online:

1. Build a Comprehensive Portfolio: Your portfolio is a visual representation of your skills and expertise. Create a comprehensive and well-organized portfolio that highlights your best work. Include a diverse range of projects

that demonstrate your versatility and capabilities. Arrange your portfolio in a logical and intuitive manner, making it easy for visitors to navigate and explore your work. Provide concise descriptions for each project, outlining the objectives, challenges, and solutions you delivered.

2. Utilize Visual Content: Visual content is highly engaging and can effectively capture the attention of your audience. Incorporate high-quality images, videos, or interactive elements into your portfolio to showcase your work. If applicable, provide before-and-after examples, interactive demos, or case studies that highlight your problem-solving skills and the impact of your work. Visual content helps potential clients visualize the value you can bring to their projects.

3. Include Client Testimonials and Reviews: Client testimonials and reviews are powerful social proof that validates your skills and professionalism. Reach out to satisfied clients and request their feedback and testimonials. Showcase these testimonials prominently on your website, social media profiles, and portfolio. Consider including client logos or linking to the actual projects you completed for added credibility.

4. Guest Blogging and Thought Leadership: Establish yourself as an industry expert by guest blogging on reputable websites or publishing insightful articles on your own blog. Share your expertise, experiences, and tips related to your niche. This demonstrates your knowledge and positions you as a thought leader in your field. Engage with the readers by responding to comments and encouraging discussions. This exposure can attract potential clients who value your expertise.

5. Participate in Industry Events and Competitions: Engaging in industry events, conferences, and competitions provides excellent opportunities to showcase your work and expertise. Present your projects, speak at panels, or contribute to discussions related to your field. Participating in such events helps you establish credibility, expand your network, and gain exposure to potential clients and collaborators.

6. Offer Free Resources and Samples: Provide valuable free resources, such as e-books, templates, or tools, that demonstrate your expertise and provide value to your audience. This not only establishes your credibility but also helps build trust and goodwill. Offer free samples or trial versions of your services to give potential clients a taste of what you can deliver. This allows them to experience the quality of your work firsthand.

7. Collaborate and Contribute to Open Source Projects: Collaborating on open-source projects or contributing to community initiatives is an excellent way to showcase your skills and expertise. It demonstrates your ability to work in a

team, contribute to larger projects, and solve complex problems. Open-source contributions also help you gain recognition within the industry and expand your professional network.

8. Stay Active on Professional Platforms: Regularly update your professional profiles, such as LinkedIn, Behance, or Dribbble, with your latest work and accomplishments. Engage with relevant communities, join industry-specific groups, and participate in discussions. Actively sharing your work and expertise on these platforms increases your visibility and attracts potential clients who are actively seeking freelancers.

By effectively showcasing your work and expertise online, you establish credibility, build trust, and attract clients who value your skills. Regularly update and expand your portfolio, engage in thought leadership activities, and actively participate in industry events to ensure your online presence reflects your current capabilities and accomplishments.

CHAPTER 4: FINDING FREELANCING OPPORTUNITIES

As a freelancer, finding consistent and rewarding freelancing opportunities is crucial for your success. While talent and expertise are essential, you also need to proactively seek out opportunities and effectively market your services. In this chapter, we will explore strategies and techniques for finding freelancing opportunities and securing long-term clients.

4.1 Tapping into Freelance Job Platforms

Freelance job platforms have become popular avenues for finding freelancing opportunities. These platforms connect freelancers with clients looking for specific skills or services. Here are key strategies to tap into freelance job platforms effectively:

Research and Choose the Right Platforms: There are numerous freelance job platforms available, each with its own specialties and target industries. Research different platforms to determine which ones align with your skills and niche. Consider factors such as platform reputation, user base, and the types of projects available. Focus your efforts on platforms that cater to your specific expertise and provide a good fit for your goals.

Create an Engaging Profile: Your profile on freelance job platforms is your opportunity to make a strong impression on potential clients. Craft a compelling profile that highlights your skills, experience, and unique value proposition. Clearly articulate the services you offer and the value you can bring to clients. Use keywords that potential clients are likely to search for when looking for freelancers in your field.

Optimize Your Portfolio: Your portfolio is a critical component of your profile on freelance job platforms. Ensure that your portfolio showcases your best work and demonstrates your expertise. Choose projects that are relevant to the types of jobs you are targeting. Provide clear descriptions and include any client feedback or testimonials you have received. Regularly update your portfolio to reflect your latest work and achievements.

Actively Search and Apply for Projects: Take an active approach in searching for projects on freelance job platforms. Regularly browse through the available opportunities and filter them based on your skills and preferences. Tailor your applications to each project, showcasing how your expertise aligns with the client's needs. Personalize your cover letters or proposals to demonstrate that you have thoroughly understood the project requirements.

Maintain Professionalism and Timeliness: When interacting with clients on freelance job platforms, professionalism is key. Respond promptly to messages, clarify any doubts, and provide accurate information. Be transparent about your availability, pricing, and project timelines. Deliver high-quality work within the agreed-upon deadlines. Building a reputation for professionalism and reliability can lead to repeat business and positive client feedback.

4.2 Networking and Building Connections

Networking and building connections are vital for finding freelancing opportunities. By expanding your professional network, you increase your chances of getting referrals, finding hidden job opportunities, and building long-term relationships with clients. Here are some strategies for effective networking:

Attend Industry Events: Attend conferences, workshops, and industry events relevant to your field. These events provide opportunities to connect with peers, industry experts, and potential clients. Engage in conversations, exchange business cards, and follow up with new contacts afterward. Participate in panel discussions or speaking engagements to showcase your expertise and gain visibility.

Join Professional Associations or Organizations: Become a member of professional associations or organizations in your industry. These groups offer networking events, workshops, and forums where you can connect with like-minded professionals. Contribute to discussions, share insights, and actively engage in the community. Networking within these associations can lead to valuable connections and potential job opportunities.

Utilize Online Networking Platforms: Online networking platforms like LinkedIn and industry-specific forums provide opportunities to connect with professionals worldwide. Build a compelling LinkedIn profile that highlights your skills and experience. Connect with colleagues, clients, and industry influencers. Engage in discussions, share valuable content, and actively participate in groups related to your field.

Request Referrals and Recommendations: Reach out to your existing clients, colleagues, and contacts and request referrals or recommendations. Satisfied clients can refer you to their networks, providing valuable leads for new projects. Recommendations on platforms like LinkedIn can also enhance your credibility and attract potential clients.

Collaborate with Peers: Collaborating with other freelancers or professionals in complementary fields can expand your reach and open up new opportunities. Partner with freelancers who offer different skills or services but serve similar clients. Jointly market your services, refer clients to each other, or collaborate on projects. Building a network of trusted collaborators can help you access a broader client base and find larger projects.

4.3 Approaching Potential Clients

Approaching potential clients directly is another effective strategy for finding freelancing opportunities. While it requires proactive outreach, it allows you to target specific clients and industries that align with your skills and interests. Here are some tips for approaching potential clients:

Research and Identify Ideal Clients: Start by researching and identifying potential clients who could benefit from your services. Consider factors such as industry, company size, location, and specific needs. Look for clients who have a track record of hiring freelancers or who may have a need for your expertise based on their projects or business objectives.

Personalize Your Approach: When reaching out to potential clients, personalize your communication to demonstrate that you have done your homework. Reference specific projects they have undertaken or challenges they may be facing. Show an understanding of their industry or market and explain how your skills and expertise can address their needs.

Craft a Compelling Introduction: Your initial contact with a potential client should be engaging and concise. Craft a compelling introduction that clearly communicates who you are, what services you offer, and the value you can provide. Highlight any relevant experience or success stories that demonstrate your capabilities. Keep your message focused, professional, and free from generic templates.

Utilize Multiple Communication Channels: Use a combination of communication channels to reach potential clients, such as email, social media, or even direct mail. Choose the channels that are most likely to resonate with your target clients. Be respectful of their preferred communication methods and follow any guidelines they have provided.

Follow Up Strategically: In many cases, a single outreach attempt may not be enough to secure a freelancing opportunity. Follow up with potential clients strategically, but avoid being pushy or overly persistent. Give them time to review your proposal or consider your services. Send a polite follow-up message or schedule a follow-up call to gauge their interest and address any questions or concerns they may have.

4.4 Creating Compelling Proposals and Bids

When responding to job postings or client inquiries, creating compelling proposals and bids is essential for standing out from the competition. A well-crafted proposal demonstrates your understanding of the client's needs and presents your skills and approach in a persuasive manner. Here are key tips for creating compelling proposals and bids:

Thoroughly Understand the Project Requirements: Before creating your proposal, take the time to thoroughly understand the client's requirements. Read the project description or brief carefully, and ask clarifying questions if needed. Ensure that you have a clear understanding of the deliverables, timeline, budget, and any other specifications.

Address the Client's Needs: Tailor your proposal to address the specific needs outlined by the client. Clearly articulate how your skills, experience, and approach align with their requirements. Explain how you can solve their problems or help them achieve their goals. Use language that demonstrates your expertise and confidence in delivering high-quality results.

Provide Relevant Samples or Case Studies: Include relevant samples of your work or case studies that demonstrate your capabilities. Choose examples that closely align with the client's project or industry. Highlight the challenges you faced, the solutions you implemented, and the results you achieved. This tangible evidence helps the client visualize the value you can bring to their project.

Outline Your Approach and Methodology: Detail your approach and methodology for completing the project. Break down the major steps, milestones, or phases involved. Explain how you will communicate and collaborate with the client throughout the process. A well-defined and transparent approach instills confidence in the client that you have a clear plan for executing the project successfully.

Provide a Competitive Pricing Structure: Your pricing should be competitive while reflecting the value you bring to the client. Clearly outline your pricing structure, whether it's an hourly rate, project-based fee, or retainer model. Justify your pricing by highlighting the expertise, quality, and level of service you offer. Consider offering different packages or options to provide flexibility to the client.

Include a Professional and Polished Presentation: Ensure that your proposal is well-presented and free from errors or typos. Use a professional template or design that aligns with your branding. Format your proposal in a logical and easy-to-read manner, using headings, bullet points, and visuals to enhance clarity. Proofread your proposal before submitting it to the client.

Follow Up and Address Questions: After submitting your proposal or bid, follow up with the client to confirm receipt and offer any further assistance. If the client has questions or requests for clarification, respond promptly and comprehensively. Be proactive in addressing any concerns and showcasing your commitment to delivering exceptional results.

4.5 Securing Long-Term Clients and Repeat Business

Securing long-term clients and repeat business is crucial for sustaining a successful freelancing career. Cultivating strong relationships with clients can lead to ongoing projects, referrals, and a steady stream of income. Here are some strategies for securing long-term clients:

Deliver Exceptional Results: Consistently deliver high-quality work that exceeds client expectations. Strive for excellence in every project you undertake. Meet project deadlines, communicate proactively, and go the extra mile to add value. By consistently delivering exceptional results, you build trust and establish yourself as a reliable and valuable partner.

Communicate Effectively: Effective communication is key to building strong client relationships. Be responsive, attentive, and proactive in your communication. Keep clients informed about project progress, changes, or any challenges you may encounter. Listen actively to their feedback and address any concerns promptly. Good communication fosters trust and ensures that expectations are aligned.

Offer Additional Value: Look for opportunities to provide additional value to your clients. Offer suggestions, insights, or improvements that can enhance their projects or processes. Anticipate their needs and offer solutions or recommendations proactively. By going above and beyond, you demonstrate your commitment to the client's success and solidify your position as a valuable partner.

Maintain Regular Contact: Stay in touch with your clients even when you are not actively working on a project. Send occasional updates, relevant industry news, or resources that may be of interest to them. This helps you stay top of mind and reinforces your relationship. Regular contact also provides opportunities for discussing potential future projects or collaborations.

Ask for Feedback and Testimonials: Request feedback from your clients upon project completion. Ask for their honest assessment of your work, communication, and overall experience. Use this feedback to continuously improve and refine your services. Positive feedback can be used as testimonials on your website or portfolio, further enhancing your credibility and attracting new clients.

Offer Incentives for Repeat Business: Consider offering incentives to encourage repeat business. This could include discounted rates for ongoing projects or special packages for retainer clients. Loyalty programs or referral bonuses can also incentivize clients to refer you to their contacts. Demonstrating appreciation for their continued business can strengthen client loyalty and encourage long-term partnerships.

Finding freelancing opportunities and securing long-term clients require a combination of proactive effort, effective communication, and a focus on delivering exceptional results. By leveraging freelance job platforms, networking, approaching potential clients, creating compelling proposals, and cultivating strong client relationships, you can establish a steady stream of projects and build a thriving freelancing career. Stay persistent, refine your strategies, and continuously improve your skills to maximize your freelancing success.

CHAPTER 5: MASTERING CLIENT COMMUNICATION

Effective communication with clients is a fundamental skill for every successful freelancer. Clear and efficient communication ensures that projects run smoothly, expectations are met, and relationships are built on trust and understanding. In this chapter, we will explore strategies and techniques for mastering client communication.

5.1 Effective Communication Strategies

Effective communication is the cornerstone of successful freelancing. It involves not only expressing yourself clearly but also actively listening and understanding your clients' needs. Here are some strategies to enhance your communication skills:

Active Listening: Actively listen to your clients to gain a deep understanding of their requirements and expectations. Pay attention to both verbal and non-verbal cues. Take notes during discussions to ensure that you capture all relevant details. Repeat back or summarize what the client has said to demonstrate your understanding.

Clarity and Conciseness: Communicate your thoughts and ideas clearly and concisely. Avoid jargon or technical terms that clients may not understand. Use simple and straightforward language to ensure that your message is easily comprehensible. Break down complex concepts into easily digestible explanations.

Timely and Responsive Communication: Respond to client messages promptly and keep them informed of project progress. Even if you don't have an immediate answer, acknowledge their message and let them know when they can expect a response. Regularly update clients on milestones, deliverables, and any changes or delays that may arise.

Choose the Right Communication Channels: Use communication channels that are convenient and preferred by your clients. This could include email, phone calls, video conferences, or project management tools. Adapt to your clients' communication preferences to ensure effective and seamless collaboration.

Professionalism and Etiquette: Maintain a professional tone in all your communications. Use proper grammar, spelling, and punctuation. Address clients respectfully and courteously. Avoid confrontational or defensive language, even in challenging situations. Treat all client interactions with professionalism and integrity.

5.2 Setting Clear Expectations

Setting clear expectations from the outset of a project is vital for avoiding misunderstandings and ensuring client satisfaction. By establishing clear guidelines and parameters, you can align your work with client expectations. Here's how to set clear expectations:

Project Scope and Deliverables: Clearly define the scope of the project and the specific deliverables that you will provide. Outline the objectives, tasks, and outcomes that the client can expect. Be specific about what is included and excluded in the scope of your work to manage client expectations effectively.

Timeline and Milestones: Establish a realistic timeline for the project and communicate it to the client. Break down the project into milestones or phases and provide estimated completion dates for each. Set clear expectations regarding the client's involvement and any dependencies required from their end.

Communication Frequency: Agree on the frequency and method of communication. Let the client know how often you will provide updates, progress reports, or check-ins. Establish regular communication touchpoints to keep the client informed and address any questions or concerns.

Revision and Approval Process: Clarify the process for revisions and approvals. Define the number of revisions included in your services and the procedure for requesting changes. Specify how approvals will be obtained and the timeline for providing feedback.

Availability and Response Time: Communicate your availability and response time to the client. Let them know the hours during which you will be accessible and how quickly they can expect a response. If you have specific days or times when you are not available, make that clear to manage expectations.

5.3 Managing Client Feedback and Revisions

Client feedback and revisions are an integral part of freelancing projects. Effectively managing client feedback ensures that their requirements are met while maintaining project momentum. Here's how to handle client feedback and revisions professionally:

Open-Mindedness: Approach client feedback with an open mind and a willingness to consider their perspective. Remember that the client's feedback is an opportunity

for improvement and alignment with their vision. Avoid being defensive and be receptive to their suggestions.

Clarify and Seek Specifics: When clients provide feedback, seek clarification to fully understand their expectations. Ask probing questions to get to the heart of their concerns or requests. Encourage clients to provide specific examples or details that can guide your revisions.

Provide Alternative Solutions: If you believe that the client's feedback may not align with the project goals or objectives, provide alternative solutions or suggestions. Offer your professional expertise and insights to help the client make informed decisions.

Manage Expectations: Clearly communicate the boundaries of your services regarding revisions. If the client's feedback exceeds the agreed-upon scope, discuss additional charges or adjustments to the project timeline. Set realistic expectations for the extent of revisions that can be accommodated.

Maintain Professionalism: Respond to client feedback in a professional and respectful manner, regardless of whether you agree with their suggestions or not. Use constructive language and avoid becoming defensive. Remember that your goal is to find a solution that satisfies the client while ensuring the project's success.

5.4 Handling Difficult Clients

Dealing with difficult clients can be challenging but is a part of freelancing. By adopting the right mindset and employing effective strategies, you can navigate challenging situations and maintain professionalism. Here are some tips for handling difficult clients:

Remain Calm and Composed: Stay calm and composed when dealing with difficult clients. Avoid responding impulsively or emotionally. Take a step back, assess the situation objectively, and respond thoughtfully. Remember that maintaining professionalism is key to resolving issues effectively.

Active Listening and Empathy: Listen attentively to understand the client's concerns or frustrations. Empathize with their perspective and acknowledge their feelings. By demonstrating that you understand their point of view, you can de-escalate tension and establish a basis for finding a resolution.

Clarify Expectations: If the difficulty arises from misaligned expectations, reiterate the agreed-upon scope, deliverables, and timelines. Remind the client of the initial discussions and any documented agreements. This can help realign expectations and find common ground.

Seek Common Ground: Identify areas of agreement or shared objectives with the client. Find common ground to build upon and focus on areas where you can collaborate positively. By highlighting shared goals, you can shift the focus away from the difficulties and work towards finding solutions.

Offer Solutions: Propose constructive solutions to address the client's concerns. Offer alternatives or compromises that meet their needs while also considering your capabilities and limitations. Collaborate with the client to find mutually beneficial solutions.

Involve a Third Party if Necessary: In situations where communication has become challenging or unproductive, consider involving a neutral third party, such as a project manager or mediator. A fresh perspective can help facilitate effective communication and find a resolution that satisfies both parties.

Know When to Walk Away: Despite your best efforts, some client relationships may become toxic or unmanageable. If a client consistently undermines your professionalism, fails to respect boundaries, or engages in abusive behavior, it may be necessary to terminate the working relationship in the best interest of your well-being and reputation.

5.5 Building Long-Term Relationships

Building long-term relationships with clients is invaluable for freelancers. Repeat business from satisfied clients not only provides stability but can also lead to referrals and positive testimonials. Here are some strategies for fostering long-term client relationships:

Consistent Communication: Maintain regular communication with your clients, even when you are not actively working on a project together. Share relevant industry news, insights, or resources that may be of interest to them. Check-in periodically to see how they are doing and if they have any upcoming projects or needs.

Exceed Expectations: Consistently deliver exceptional results that exceed client expectations. Go the extra mile to add value and demonstrate your commitment to their success

. By consistently providing high-quality work and exceptional service, you build trust and foster long-term loyalty.

Proactive Problem-Solving: Anticipate and address potential issues or challenges before they become problems. Be proactive in identifying solutions and offering suggestions to improve processes or outcomes. Position yourself as a reliable and trusted partner who is invested in the client's success.

Continual Professional Development: Stay updated on industry trends, technologies, and best practices. Continually enhance your skills and knowledge to offer added value to your clients. Demonstrate a commitment to your professional growth, which reassures clients that they are working with a competent and reliable freelancer.

Ask for Feedback and Act on It: Regularly seek feedback from your clients upon project completion. Ask for their honest assessment of your work, communication, and overall experience. Use their feedback to improve and refine your services. Act on constructive criticism and continually strive to enhance your client experience.

Client Appreciation: Show gratitude and appreciation for your clients' trust and partnership. Thank them for their business and acknowledge their contributions to your freelancing success. Consider sending personalized notes or small tokens of appreciation to celebrate milestones or express your gratitude.

Mastering client communication is essential for building a successful freelancing career. By employing effective communication strategies, setting clear expectations, managing client feedback, handling difficult situations professionally, and building long-term relationships, you can foster strong client connections and establish a solid reputation.

CHAPTER 6: PRICING AND NEGOTIATION

Pricing your services appropriately and negotiating fair contracts are crucial aspects of freelancing. The way you set your rates and handle negotiations can greatly impact your earning potential and the overall success of your freelancing career. In this chapter, we will explore strategies for pricing your services, negotiating contracts, upselling, and managing payment processes.

6.1 Understanding Freelancing Rates and Pricing Models

Setting the right rates for your freelance services requires a careful balance between your skills, experience, market demand, and the value you provide to clients. Understanding different pricing models can help you make informed decisions. Here are some common freelancing rates and pricing models to consider:

Hourly Rate: Many freelancers charge an hourly rate for their services. This model is straightforward, as you calculate your rate based on the number of hours worked. Consider factors such as your expertise, overhead costs, and the industry average when determining your hourly rate. Keep in mind that an hourly rate may not always reflect the true value you bring to a project.

Project-Based Pricing: Instead of charging by the hour, you can offer fixed project-based pricing. This approach involves quoting a flat fee for the entire project. Consider the scope, complexity, and estimated time commitment required for the project when determining your project-based price. It's important to accurately assess the project's requirements to avoid underestimating the effort involved.

Value-Based Pricing: Value-based pricing focuses on the value you deliver to the client rather than the time or effort invested. This model considers the impact of your work on the client's business or bottom line. It requires a deep understanding of the client's needs and the outcomes they seek. Value-based pricing allows you to charge higher rates for specialized or high-impact services.

Retainer Pricing: Retainers involve establishing an ongoing agreement with a client for a set period. The client pays a fixed fee in advance to secure your availability and a certain number of hours or services each month. Retainers provide stability and predictable income, particularly for long-term client relationships.

Hybrid Models: You can also create hybrid pricing models that combine different approaches. For example, you may charge an upfront fee for project initiation and planning, followed by an hourly rate or project-based pricing for the execution phase. Hybrid models allow for flexibility and customization to meet both your needs and the client's requirements.

Market Research: Before setting your rates, conduct market research to understand the prevailing rates in your industry and niche. Consider factors such as your experience level, expertise, and the value you bring to clients when positioning yourself in the market. Pricing too high may lead to fewer opportunities, while pricing too low may undervalue your skills and efforts.

6.2 Negotiating Fair Contracts and Rates

Negotiating contracts and rates is a common part of the freelancing process. Effective negotiation allows you to secure fair terms and compensation for your work. Here are some tips for successful negotiation:

Research and Preparation: Before entering into negotiations, research the client, industry standards, and the project requirements. Understand the client's needs, objectives, and budget constraints. Prepare a clear justification for your rates and the value you provide. This preparation will help you enter negotiations with confidence.

Define Your Non-Negotiables: Determine your non-negotiables before entering negotiations. These are the terms or conditions that you consider essential for your work. It could be your minimum acceptable rate, project timeline, or scope of work. Knowing your non-negotiables helps you maintain boundaries and negotiate from a position of strength.

Anchor High: When discussing rates or pricing, start the negotiation with a slightly higher figure than what you expect to receive. This technique, known as anchoring, allows room for negotiation and gives you the opportunity to reach a more favorable outcome. However, be prepared to justify the value you bring and provide evidence of your expertise.

Focus on Value: Emphasize the value you bring to the project and the potential impact on the client's business. Shift the conversation away from price alone and highlight the results and benefits they can expect from working with you. By highlighting value, you can justify higher rates and negotiate based on the outcomes you deliver.

Seek Win-Win Solutions: Negotiation is not about one party winning and the other losing. Aim for a win-win outcome where both you and the client feel satisfied with the terms. Look for creative solutions that address the client's needs while ensuring fair compensation and favorable conditions for your work.

Contract Terms: Carefully review and negotiate the contract terms to protect your interests. Pay attention to payment terms, project scope, deliverables, revisions, intellectual property rights, confidentiality, and termination clauses. Seek professional advice if needed, especially for complex or high-value projects.

Negotiating Scope Creep: Scope creep refers to the gradual expansion of project requirements beyond the initial agreement. Clearly define the scope of work and communicate any additional charges or revisions for out-of-scope requests. Handle scope creep discussions professionally, suggesting alternative solutions or proposing a change order to accommodate the new requirements.

6.3 Upselling and Adding Value to Your Services

Upselling involves offering additional services or enhancements to your existing clients. It allows you to increase your revenue while providing added value to your clients. Here are some strategies for upselling and adding value to your services:

Identify Client Needs: Continuously assess your clients' needs and identify areas where you can provide additional value. Consider their business objectives, pain points, and challenges. Proactively suggest services or solutions that can help them achieve their goals or overcome obstacles.

Package Your Services: Create packages or bundles that combine different services or offer a comprehensive solution to your clients. Packaging your services simplifies the decision-making process for clients and encourages them to opt for a more extensive engagement.

Offer Tiered Pricing: Develop tiered pricing structures that cater to different client budgets and requirements. By offering multiple options, you provide flexibility and accommodate a broader range of clients. Each tier can offer different levels of service or additional features.

Educate and Inform: Share your expertise and insights with clients through blog posts, newsletters, or educational resources. Demonstrate your knowledge and provide valuable information that can help clients make informed decisions. This positions you as a trusted advisor and increases the perceived value of your services.

Cross-Selling and Referrals: Leverage your existing client relationships to cross-sell your services. If you offer complementary services, inform your clients about the additional ways you can assist them. Additionally, ask satisfied clients for referrals to expand your network and reach new potential clients.

6.4 Handling Payment and Invoicing

Efficient payment and invoicing processes are crucial for maintaining cash flow and ensuring timely compensation for your work. Here are some best practices for handling payment and invoicing:

Clear Payment Terms: Establish clear payment terms and communicate them to clients upfront. Specify the preferred payment method, currency, and payment schedule. Include this information in your contract or agreement to set expectations from the beginning.

Professional Invoices: Create professional and detailed invoices for your clients. Include your business name, contact information, client details, a breakdown of services provided, rates, and the total amount due. Clearly state the payment due date and any late payment fees or penalties.

Invoice Tracking: Keep track of your invoices, including the date sent, payment due date, and payment status. Utilize accounting software or online tools to streamline the invoicing process and automate reminders for overdue payments.

Prompt Invoicing: Send invoices promptly upon project completion or according to the agreed-upon payment schedule. Prompt invoicing sets clear expectations and signals your professionalism. Avoid delays in invoicing to expedite payment processing.

Payment Options: Provide multiple payment options to accommodate your client preferences. Accept online payments, credit cards, bank transfers, or other secure and convenient methods. Clearly outline the accepted payment methods on your invoices and website.

Follow Up on Late Payments: If a client misses a payment deadline, follow up promptly with a polite reminder. Maintain open communication and inquire about any issues or concerns they may have. Handle late payments professionally but assertively to ensure timely resolution.

Building a successful freelancing career requires effective pricing strategies, skilled negotiation, upselling tactics, and efficient payment processes. By understanding different pricing models, negotiating fair contracts, adding value to your services, and implementing streamlined payment and invoicing procedures, you can optimize your earning potential and establish a strong financial foundation.

CHAPTER 7: TIME MANAGEMENT AND PRODUCTIVITY

Effective time management and productivity are vital skills for freelancers. Being able to prioritize tasks, meet deadlines, and maintain a healthy work-life balance are key factors in achieving success in your freelancing career. In this chapter, we will explore strategies to help you manage your time efficiently and enhance your productivity.

7.1 Setting Priorities and Deadlines

Setting priorities and deadlines is essential for effective time management. By understanding the importance and urgency of your tasks, you can allocate your time and resources accordingly. Here are some tips for setting priorities and deadlines:

Identify High-Priority Tasks: Start by identifying tasks that are crucial to the success of your projects or have imminent deadlines. These tasks should align with your clients' objectives and directly contribute to your overall goals. Focus your energy on completing these high-priority tasks first.

Consider Importance and Urgency: When assessing tasks, consider both their importance and urgency. Important tasks contribute to long-term goals, while urgent tasks require immediate attention. Prioritize tasks that are both important and urgent, as they have the highest impact on your progress.

Break Down Large Tasks: Large projects or tasks can be overwhelming. Break them down into smaller, more manageable subtasks. This allows you to work on them incrementally, making progress and staying motivated along the way.

Set Realistic Deadlines: When assigning deadlines to tasks, be realistic in your estimations. Consider the complexity of the task, your availability, and potential obstacles that may arise. Avoid overcommitting and setting unrealistic expectations, as it can lead to unnecessary stress and compromised quality.

Utilize Time Management Techniques: Explore various time management techniques, such as the Pomodoro Technique, time blocking, or the Eisenhower Matrix. These techniques can help you allocate time effectively, increase focus, and reduce distractions.

Regularly Review and Adjust: Regularly review your priorities and deadlines to ensure they are still relevant and aligned with your current goals. Adjustments may be necessary as project requirements change or new opportunities arise.

7.2 Creating Effective Work Schedules

Creating a well-structured work schedule can significantly improve your productivity. By establishing a routine and allocating dedicated time for specific tasks, you can optimize your workflow. Consider the following tips for creating an effective work schedule:

Define Your Most Productive Hours: Identify the times of day when you feel most energized and focused. This is when you should schedule your most critical and demanding tasks. Aligning your work with your natural energy patterns can enhance your productivity.

Establish Regular Work Hours: Set consistent work hours to establish a routine and create a sense of structure. This helps you stay disciplined and maintain a professional work mindset. Communicate your availability to clients and stakeholders to manage expectations.

Allocate Time for Administrative Tasks: In addition to client work, allocate time for administrative tasks such as invoicing, responding to emails, and organizing your files. By dedicating specific time slots for these activities, you can prevent them from encroaching on your productive work time.

Block Distraction-Free Time: Identify periods when you can work without interruptions or distractions. During these blocks, turn off notifications, close unnecessary tabs or applications, and create a focused work environment. Use tools like website blockers or time management apps to minimize distractions.

Allow for Flexibility: While having a schedule is important, allow for flexibility to accommodate unexpected circumstances or changes in project requirements. Embrace adaptability and build in buffer time for unforeseen tasks or emergencies.

7.3 Overcoming Procrastination

Procrastination can be a major obstacle to productivity. Overcoming procrastination requires discipline, self-awareness, and effective strategies. Here are some techniques to help you overcome procrastination:

Identify Procrastination Triggers: Reflect on what triggers your procrastination tendencies. It could be fear of

failure, feeling overwhelmed, or simply a lack of interest in a particular task. Once you understand your triggers, you can develop strategies to address them.

Break Tasks into Smaller Steps: Large or complex tasks can feel daunting and lead to procrastination. Break them down into smaller, more manageable steps. Focus on completing one step at a time, which makes the task less overwhelming and more achievable.

Set Clear Goals: Set clear, specific goals for each task or project. Clearly define what needs to be accomplished and establish a deadline. Visualize the end result and remind yourself of the satisfaction and rewards that come from completing the task.

Eliminate Distractions: Identify and eliminate distractions that contribute to procrastination. Create a dedicated work environment that is free from distractions like social media, television, or personal obligations. Use productivity tools that block websites or limit your access to distractions during work sessions.

Practice Time Boxing: Time boxing involves allocating a specific amount of time to work on a task without interruption. Set a timer for a predetermined period, such as 25 minutes, and work on the task until the timer goes off. Take short breaks between time boxes to recharge.

Utilize Accountability Techniques: Hold yourself accountable by sharing your goals and progress with an accountability partner or joining a mastermind group. Having someone to check in with regularly can provide motivation and support in overcoming procrastination.

Reward Yourself: Create a system of rewards for completing tasks or reaching milestones. Celebrate your accomplishments, whether it's taking a short break, treating yourself to something you enjoy, or engaging in a favorite hobby. Rewards can serve as incentives and increase motivation.

7.4 Managing Multiple Projects and Clients

As a freelancer, it's common to juggle multiple projects and clients simultaneously. Efficiently managing your workload and maintaining high-quality output is crucial. Consider the following strategies for managing multiple projects and clients effectively:

Prioritize and Plan: Assess the priorities and deadlines for each project and client. Identify the most critical tasks and allocate your time accordingly. Create a project plan or task list that outlines the steps required for each project, allowing you to stay organized and focused.

Communicate and Set Expectations: Maintain open communication with your clients regarding your availability, project timelines, and progress. Set realistic expectations regarding response times, deliverables, and any potential limitations due to your workload. Transparency and proactive communication build trust and understanding.

Use Project Management Tools: Implement project management tools or software to streamline your workflow and keep track of project progress. These tools help you organize tasks, collaborate with clients or team members, set deadlines, and monitor project timelines.

Delegate or Outsource: If possible, delegate certain tasks or consider outsourcing to specialized professionals or freelancers. Delegating less critical or time-consuming tasks can free up your time to focus on high-priority work and ensure efficient project management.

Time Blocking: Utilize time blocking techniques to allocate dedicated time for each project or client. Create time blocks on your schedule to work on specific projects, allowing for focused and uninterrupted work sessions.

Maintain Clear Communication Channels: Ensure that you have established clear communication channels with each client. This includes email, project management platforms, instant messaging apps, or video conferencing tools. Streamlined communication helps you stay updated and accessible to clients while managing multiple projects.

Regularly Assess Workload: Regularly evaluate your workload and assess your capacity to take on additional projects. Avoid overcommitting and be mindful of your limits. Consider your work-life balance and ensure that you can maintain a high standard of work without compromising your well-being.

7.5 Maintaining a Healthy Work-Life Balance

Maintaining a healthy work-life balance is essential for your overall well-being and long-term success as a freelancer. Here are some strategies to help you achieve and maintain a healthy work-life balance:

Set Boundaries: Establish

 clear boundaries between your work and personal life. Define specific work hours and communicate them to your clients and stakeholders. Respect your personal time and prioritize self-care, hobbies, and spending time with loved ones.

Take Regular Breaks: Allow yourself regular breaks throughout the workday to rest, recharge, and prevent burnout. Step away from your workspace, engage in physical activity, practice mindfulness, or pursue activities that bring you joy. Breaks can enhance productivity and overall well-being.

Create Separate Workspaces: If possible, designate a separate workspace for your freelancing activities. Having a dedicated workspace helps create a physical separation between work and personal life, allowing you to mentally switch off when you're not working.

Practice Self-Care: Prioritize self-care activities such as exercise, healthy eating, quality sleep, and relaxation techniques. Engage in activities that reduce stress and promote physical and mental well-being. Remember that taking care of yourself is crucial for maintaining productivity and creativity.

Set Realistic Expectations: Avoid the temptation to overwork or constantly be available to clients. Set realistic expectations regarding your availability, response times, and project deadlines. Communicate your boundaries clearly and stick to them.

Learn to Say No: It's important to recognize your limitations and learn to say no when necessary. Be selective about the projects and clients you take on, ensuring they align with your values, expertise, and availability. Saying no allows you to focus on high-quality work and maintain a healthy work-life balance.

Seek Support and Connection: Connect with other freelancers or professionals in your field to share experiences, advice, and support. Join online communities, attend networking events, or participate in industry-related groups. Building connections can provide valuable insights and a sense of belonging.

By implementing effective time management techniques, setting priorities and deadlines, creating work schedules, overcoming procrastination, managing multiple projects and clients, and maintaining a healthy work-life balance, you can maximize your productivity and achieve sustainable success as a freelancer.

CHAPTER 8: ENHANCING YOUR SKILLS AND EXPERTISE

In the fast-paced and ever-evolving world of freelancing, it's crucial to continuously enhance your skills and expertise. By investing in continuous learning, mastering new tools and technologies, expanding your service offerings, collaborating with other freelancers, and staying ahead of industry trends, you can position yourself as a valuable and sought-after professional. In this chapter, we will explore strategies to help you enhance your skills and expertise as a freelancer.

8.1 Continuous Learning and Professional Development

Continuous learning and professional development are essential for freelancers to stay relevant and competitive in their respective fields. Here are some strategies to foster continuous learning:

Stay Updated with Industry News: Stay informed about the latest trends, developments, and innovations in your industry. Follow industry blogs, subscribe to relevant newsletters, and participate in online forums or communities. Regularly engage in conversations and discussions to broaden your knowledge and perspectives.

Attend Workshops, Webinars, and Conferences: Participate in workshops, webinars, and conferences that provide opportunities for skill development and knowledge sharing. These events often feature industry experts and thought leaders who can provide valuable insights and practical advice.

Take Online Courses: Online learning platforms offer a wealth of courses and tutorials on a wide range of topics. Invest in relevant courses to expand your skill set, deepen your expertise, or learn new technologies. Online courses provide flexibility and convenience, allowing you to learn at your own pace.

Join Professional Associations: Consider joining professional associations or organizations related to your industry. These associations often provide access to resources, networking opportunities, and professional development programs. Engage in their events, webinars, and workshops to enhance your knowledge and build connections.

Seek Mentors and Coaches: Connect with experienced professionals who can serve as mentors or coaches. They can provide guidance, share their experiences, and offer valuable advice to help you navigate your freelancing journey. Mentors and coaches can accelerate your learning process and provide valuable insights.

Embrace Feedback: Actively seek feedback from clients, colleagues, and peers. Embrace constructive criticism as an opportunity for growth and improvement. Analyze feedback to identify areas where you can enhance your skills and make adjustments accordingly.

8.2 Mastering New Tools and Technologies

Technology plays a significant role in the freelancing landscape, and staying updated with new tools and technologies is crucial for success. Here's how you can master new tools and technologies:

Stay Informed: Keep up with emerging tools, software, and technologies relevant to your industry. Follow technology news, read industry publications, and subscribe to blogs or podcasts that focus on the latest advancements. Awareness is the first step towards mastery.

Explore Online Resources: Take advantage of online resources such as tutorials, videos, and documentation provided by software and tool developers. Many tools offer knowledge bases, user forums, and support communities where you can learn from experts and fellow users.

Hands-on Practice: The best way to master new tools and technologies is through hands-on practice. Allocate dedicated time to experiment with new tools, explore their features, and understand their functionalities. Create sample projects or scenarios to apply what you learn.

Take Advantage of Training Materials: Many software and tool developers offer training materials such as online courses, webinars, or documentation to help users master their products. Take advantage of these resources to deepen your understanding and proficiency.

Collaborate and Learn from Others: Connect with other freelancers or professionals in your field to exchange knowledge and experiences related to specific tools or technologies. Participate in online communities, attend user groups, or join forums where you can learn from others and share your expertise.

8.3 Expanding Your Service Offerings

Expanding your service offerings can open new opportunities and attract a broader client base. Here are strategies to consider when expanding your service offerings:

Identify Client

Needs: Conduct market research and identify emerging trends, challenges, and demands within your industry. Understand the needs and pain points of potential clients to determine how you can address them with additional services.

Evaluate Your Skill Set: Assess your current skills and expertise to identify areas where you can expand. Consider acquiring new skills, certifications, or training to offer a wider range of services. Evaluate the feasibility of acquiring these skills based on your interests and market demand.

Collaborate with Specialists: Partner with other freelancers or professionals who specialize in complementary areas. Collaborative partnerships allow you to leverage the expertise of others and offer comprehensive solutions to clients. This can lead to larger projects and increased client satisfaction.

Upselling and Cross-Selling: When working with existing clients, identify opportunities to upsell or cross-sell additional services. If you've built a strong relationship and delivered value with your current services, clients may be more inclined to explore additional offerings from you.

Package Services: Package your services into bundled offerings that provide a comprehensive solution to clients. This simplifies the decision-making process for clients and positions you as a one-stop solution provider. Create clear and compelling packages that communicate the value of the bundled services.

Market Your New Offerings: Update your website, portfolio, and marketing materials to reflect your expanded service offerings. Clearly communicate the benefits and value of the new services to attract the attention of potential clients. Leverage your existing client base and network to promote your expanded offerings.

8.4 Collaborating and Partnering with Other Freelancers

Collaborating and partnering with other freelancers can bring numerous benefits, including access to new opportunities, shared expertise, and increased capacity. Consider the following strategies for effective collaboration:

Identify Complementary Freelancers: Identify freelancers who possess complementary skills and expertise to yours. Look for individuals whose services align with your offerings and can enhance the value you provide to clients.

Network and Build Connections: Attend industry events, join online communities, and actively network with other freelancers. Build relationships and establish connections with professionals who can become potential collaborators or partners. Engage in conversations, share insights, and offer support.

Establish Clear Roles and Expectations: When collaborating with other freelancers, establish clear roles, responsibilities, and expectations from the outset. Define project scopes, timelines, deliverables, and communication protocols to ensure a smooth collaboration process.

Communicate Effectively: Maintain open and transparent communication with your collaborators. Regularly check in, provide updates, and address any issues that may arise during the collaboration. Clear and effective communication helps align efforts and maintain project momentum.

Document Agreements: When collaborating with other freelancers, it's essential to have clear agreements in place. Document the terms of collaboration, including ownership of work, confidentiality, compensation, and dispute resolution mechanisms. Having written agreements protects all parties involved and minimizes potential conflicts.

Share Knowledge and Resources: Collaborative partnerships allow for the sharing of knowledge, resources, and best practices. Take advantage of the expertise and insights of your collaborators, and reciprocate by offering your own expertise and support. This collective knowledge can enhance the quality of work and deliver added value to clients.

8.5 Staying Ahead of Industry Trends

To remain competitive as a freelancer, staying ahead of industry trends is crucial. Here are strategies to help you stay informed and proactive:

Engage in Continuous Research: Dedicate time to conduct regular research on industry trends, emerging technologies, and changing client demands. Stay informed about the latest innovations, developments, and best practices within your field.

Follow Thought Leaders and Influencers: Identify and follow thought leaders, influencers, and industry experts in your niche. Subscribe to their blogs, newsletters, or social media channels to access their insights and expertise. Engage in conversations and discussions to deepen your understanding and stay updated.

Attend Industry Events and Conferences

: Attend industry conferences, workshops, and seminars to gain exposure to the latest trends, technologies, and thought leadership. These events provide opportunities to network with industry professionals and gain valuable insights.

Join Online Communities and Forums: Participate in online communities and forums dedicated to your industry. Engage in discussions, share insights, and learn from fellow professionals. These communities serve as valuable sources of information and can keep you abreast of industry trends.

Subscribe to Industry Publications: Subscribe to relevant industry publications, magazines, or journals to receive regular updates on industry news, trends, and case studies. These publications often feature articles written by experts, providing valuable insights and analysis.

Embrace Lifelong Learning: Cultivate a mindset of lifelong learning and professional growth. Continuously seek opportunities to acquire new skills, attend workshops or courses, and engage in self-study. Embracing continuous learning helps you adapt to industry changes and stay ahead of the curve.

By embracing continuous learning, mastering new tools and technologies, expanding your service offerings, collaborating with other freelancers, and staying ahead of industry trends, you can elevate your skills and expertise as a freelancer.

CHAPTER 9: OVERCOMING CHALLENGES AND BUILDING RESILIENCE

Freelancing, like any profession, comes with its own set of challenges. From burnout to financial management, rejection to maintaining motivation, and building a support network, it's important to develop strategies to overcome these obstacles and build resilience. In this chapter, we will explore strategies to help you navigate and overcome common challenges as a freelancer.

9.1 Dealing with Freelancer Burnout

Freelancer burnout can be a significant challenge due to the often unpredictable and demanding nature of the work. Here are strategies to help you manage and prevent burnout:

Recognize the Signs: Familiarize yourself with the signs of burnout, such as fatigue, decreased motivation, irritability, and decreased productivity. Acknowledging and addressing these signs early can help prevent burnout from escalating.

Set Boundaries: Establish clear boundaries between work and personal life. Define your working hours, take regular breaks, and allocate time for self-care and relaxation. Communicate your boundaries to clients and stakeholders to manage expectations.

Practice Self-Care: Prioritize self-care activities that promote physical, mental, and emotional well-being. Engage in activities such as exercise, meditation, hobbies, and spending time with loved ones. Taking care of yourself is essential for maintaining balance and preventing burnout.

Delegate and Outsource: Identify tasks that can be delegated or outsourced to lighten your workload. Collaborate with other freelancers, hire virtual assistants, or use automation tools to streamline your processes and free up time for more important tasks.

Manage Workload: Be mindful of your workload and avoid overcommitting yourself. Learn to say no to projects or clients that exceed your capacity. Prioritize projects and tasks, and focus on high-value activities that align with your goals and expertise.

Seek Support: Reach out to fellow freelancers or professionals in your field who can understand and relate to your experiences. Share your challenges, seek advice, and offer support to one another. Knowing that you're not alone can provide comfort and perspective.

9.2 Managing Finances and Taxes

Managing finances and taxes is an essential aspect of freelancing. Here are strategies to help you stay on top of your financial responsibilities:

Separate Personal and Business Finances: Open a separate business bank account to keep your personal and business finances separate. This helps with tracking income and expenses, simplifies tax filing, and provides a clear picture of your financial situation.

Track Income and Expenses: Maintain detailed records of your income and expenses. Use accounting software or tools to track invoices, payments, and business-related expenses. Regularly review your financial statements to monitor your cash flow and financial health.

Budgeting and Financial Planning: Create a budget to allocate funds for various expenses and financial goals. Plan for taxes, savings, investments, and emergency funds. Having a financial plan helps you make informed decisions and ensures financial stability.

Consult with a Financial Professional: Consider consulting with a financial advisor or accountant who specializes in working with freelancers. They can provide guidance on tax planning, deductions, and financial strategies tailored to your specific situation.

Stay Updated with Tax Regulations: Stay informed about tax regulations and deadlines relevant to freelancers in your jurisdiction. Be aware of deductible expenses, self-employment taxes, and any tax benefits available to freelancers. Consider using tax software or consulting with a tax professional to ensure accurate and timely tax filings.

9.3 Handling Rejection and Criticism

Rejection and criticism are inevitable aspects of freelancing. Here are strategies to help you handle them effectively:

Develop Resilience: Cultivate a resilient mindset by reframing rejection and criticism as opportunities for growth and improvement. Embrace the learning experience and use feedback constructively to enhance your skills and deliver better results.

Separate Feedback from Self-Worth: Remember that feedback and criticism are not a reflection of your worth as a person or a professional. Learn to detach your self-esteem from external opinions and focus on continuous improvement.

Seek Constructive Feedback: Actively seek constructive feedback from clients, colleagues, and mentors. Request specific feedback on your work and areas for improvement. This helps you gain valuable insights and refine your skills.

Respond Professionally: When faced with criticism, respond professionally and objectively. Avoid getting defensive or taking feedback personally. Instead, seek clarification if needed and use the feedback as an opportunity to enhance your work.

Learn from Rejection: View rejection as a stepping stone to success. Analyze the reasons behind the rejection, identify areas for improvement, and use the experience to refine your approach. Remember that every rejection brings you closer to finding the right opportunities.

Maintain Confidence: Build a strong foundation of self-belief and confidence in your abilities. Recognize your achievements, focus on your strengths, and celebrate your successes. Developing a positive mindset helps you navigate through challenges with resilience.

9.4 Maintaining Motivation and Confidence

As a freelancer, maintaining motivation and confidence is crucial for long-term success. Here are strategies to help you stay motivated and confident:

Set Meaningful Goals: Establish clear, measurable, and achievable goals for your freelancing career. Break them down into smaller milestones to track your progress and celebrate achievements along the way. Meaningful goals provide a sense of direction and purpose.

Create a Vision Board: Visualize your goals and aspirations by creating a vision board. Include images, quotes, and representations of your desired outcomes. Display it in your workspace as a reminder of what you're working towards and as a source of inspiration.

Seek Inspiration: Surround yourself with sources of inspiration. Follow industry leaders, read books, listen to podcasts, and attend webinars or conferences related to your field. Engage in activities that fuel your passion and keep you motivated.

Establish a Routine: Develop a daily routine that supports your productivity and motivation. Set specific work hours, create a dedicated workspace, and establish rituals that signal the start and end of your workday. Routines help establish a sense of structure and discipline.

Celebrate Achievements: Acknowledge and celebrate your achievements, no matter how small they may seem. Reward yourself for reaching milestones or completing challenging projects. Celebrating success reinforces a positive mindset and boosts confidence.

Seek Professional Development: Continuously invest in your professional development. Attend workshops, take online courses, and participate in training programs to enhance your skills and knowledge. Learning new things keeps your work fresh, sparks creativity, and maintains your motivation.

9.5 Building a Support Network

Building a support network is essential for freelancers. Here are strategies to help you create a supportive community:

Join Professional Associations: Explore professional associations or organizations related to your industry or niche. Joining these communities provides opportunities for networking, learning, and accessing resources. Engage in discussions, attend events, and build relationships with like-minded professionals.

Network Online and Offline: Engage in online networking through social media platforms, industry forums, and professional networking sites. Connect with fellow freelancers, potential clients, and industry influencers. Offline, attend networking events, conferences, and meetups to establish face-to-face connections.

Collaborate with Peers: Collaborate with other freelancers on projects, workshops, or events. By working together, you can leverage each other's expertise, share resources, and expand your reach. Collaborative projects also provide opportunities for mutual support and learning.

Join Mastermind Groups: Consider joining or forming a mastermind group with other freelancers. These groups meet regularly to share experiences, provide support, and offer accountability. Mastermind groups provide a safe space to discuss challenges, brainstorm ideas, and receive constructive feedback.

Mentorship and Coaching: Seek mentorship or coaching from experienced freelancers or professionals in your field. Mentors can provide guidance, share insights, and offer valuable advice based on their own experiences. Coaching sessions can help you set goals, overcome challenges, and enhance your skills.

Supportive Friends and Family: Surround yourself with friends and family who support your freelancing journey. Share your successes and challenges with them, and seek their understanding and encouragement. Their support can be invaluable in times of doubt or uncertainty.

Building a support network helps you feel connected, supported, and inspired as a freelancer. The encouragement, advice, and camaraderie within your network can contribute to your overall success and well-being.

In the next and final chapter, we will bring together all the essential elements discussed throughout this eBook and provide you with a roadmap for sustained success as a freelancer

CHAPTER 10: SUSTAINING LONG-TERM SUCCESS AS A FREELANCER

Congratulations! You've learned the fundamental principles and strategies to become a successful freelancer. In this final chapter, we will bring together all the essential elements discussed throughout this eBook and provide you with a roadmap for sustaining long-term success in your freelancing career.

10.1 Evaluating and Refining Your Freelancing Strategy

As you progress in your freelancing journey, it's essential to regularly evaluate and refine your freelancing strategy. Here are key steps to help you stay on track:

Reflect on Your Progress: Take time to reflect on your freelancing journey and assess your achievements, challenges, and areas for improvement. Review your goals and milestones, and identify any necessary adjustments to your strategy.

Adapt to Industry Changes: Stay informed about industry trends, technological advancements, and evolving client needs. Continuously adapt your skills, service offerings, and marketing approaches to remain relevant and competitive.

Seek Feedback from Clients: Request feedback from your clients to gauge their satisfaction with your work and identify areas where you can improve. Actively listen to their suggestions and implement changes to enhance your client experience.

Monitor Your Financial Performance: Regularly review your financial performance to ensure your freelancing efforts are financially viable. Analyze your revenue, expenses, and profitability to identify opportunities for growth and optimize your pricing strategies.

10.2 Expanding Your Network and Client Base

Continually expanding your network and client base is vital for sustained success. Here are strategies to help you achieve this:

Networking Events and Conferences: Attend industry events, conferences, and meetups to expand your professional network. Engage in conversations, exchange business cards, and follow up with potential clients or collaborators. Building strong relationships can lead to valuable opportunities.

Referrals and Testimonials: Leverage the power of referrals and testimonials from satisfied clients. Ask for testimonials and encourage clients to refer you to their colleagues or contacts. Positive word-of-mouth can significantly impact your credibility and attract new clients.

Content Marketing: Create valuable content through blog posts, articles, or videos that showcase your expertise. Share this content on your website, social media platforms, and industry forums to establish yourself as a thought leader. Valuable content attracts potential clients and builds trust.

Collaborate with Other Freelancers: Collaborate with other freelancers on joint projects or partnerships. By pooling your skills and networks, you can expand your reach and offer comprehensive solutions to clients. Collaborations also provide opportunities for cross-promotion and knowledge sharing.

10.3 Cultivating Client Relationships and Fostering Loyalty

Nurturing client relationships and fostering loyalty is key to long-term success as a freelancer. Here's how you can achieve this:

Excellent Communication: Maintain open, clear, and prompt communication with your clients. Respond to their inquiries, provide regular project updates, and address any concerns promptly. Good communication builds trust and shows your dedication to their success.

Deliver Exceptional Work: Consistently deliver high-quality work that exceeds your clients' expectations. Strive for excellence in every project, paying attention to detail and ensuring timely delivery. Exceptional work establishes your reputation and encourages repeat business.

Offer Value-Added Services: Look for opportunities to provide additional value to your clients. Offer suggestions, insights, or recommendations that go beyond the initial project scope. This demonstrates your expertise and commitment to their success.

Maintain Professionalism: Conduct yourself professionally in all interactions with clients. Be reliable, meet deadlines, and respect confidentiality agreements. Professionalism builds trust and fosters long-term relationships.

Regular Check-Ins: Maintain regular check-ins with your clients, even after a project is completed. Follow up to ensure their satisfaction, address any concerns, and explore future collaboration opportunities. This demonstrates your commitment to building lasting partnerships.

10.4 Embracing Continuous Learning and Growth

To sustain long-term success, it's crucial to embrace continuous learning and personal growth. Here are strategies to help you stay ahead:

Stay Updated on Industry Trends: Stay abreast of industry trends, emerging technologies, and new best practices. Subscribe to industry newsletters, follow relevant blogs, and participate in webinars or workshops. Continuous learning keeps you at the forefront of your field.

Invest in Professional Development: Continually invest in your professional development by taking courses, attending conferences, or obtaining certifications. Develop new skills, broaden your knowledge base, and explore new areas of expertise. Continuous growth enhances your value proposition.

Seek Feedback and Coaching: Actively seek feedback from clients, mentors, or peers. Embrace constructive criticism as an opportunity for improvement. Consider working with a coach or mentor who can provide guidance and support in your professional development.

Experiment and Innovate: Be open to experimenting with new approaches, tools, or techniques in your work. Embrace innovation and explore creative solutions to challenges. Embracing experimentation and innovation sets you apart from competitors.

Becoming a successful freelancer requires dedication, perseverance, and continuous learning. By building a strong foundation, establishing your online presence, finding freelancing opportunities, mastering client communication, pricing and negotiation, managing your time and productivity, enhancing your skills, overcoming challenges, and fostering resilience, you can create a thriving freelancing career.

Remember, success as a freelancer is not an overnight achievement but a journey of constant growth and improvement. Stay committed to your craft, adapt to changes, nurture client relationships, and prioritize personal and professional development. With determination and the strategies outlined in this eBook, you have the tools to become a successful freelancer and enjoy a fulfilling and prosperous career.

Good luck on your freelancing journey!

ACKNOWLEDGEMENT

Writing the eBook, "How to Become a Successful Freelancer," would not have been possible without the support and contributions of several individuals. We would like to express our heartfelt gratitude to the following:

First and foremost, we would like to thank all the freelancers who shared their experiences, insights, and expertise, which served as valuable inspiration and information for this eBook. Your stories and perspectives have truly enriched its content.

We extend our sincere appreciation to our editor, who provided invaluable guidance, feedback, and editing expertise throughout the writing process. Your attention to detail and commitment to excellence have significantly improved the quality of this eBook.

We would like to express our gratitude to our friends and family for their constant support and encouragement. Your belief in our abilities and unwavering encouragement have been instrumental in the pursuit of this project.

Lastly, we would like to thank the readers of this eBook. It is our sincere hope that the information and strategies provided within these pages will guide you on your journey to becoming a successful freelancer. Your interest and engagement in this topic inspire us to continue sharing knowledge and insights.

Thank you all for your contributions, support, and encouragement.

www.ingramcontent.com/pod-product-compliance
Lightning Source LLC
Chambersburg PA
CBHW070501220526
45466CB00004B/1918